A Pandemic Prose: A Journey of Healing Amid Disaster

Autumn Haile

BookLeaf Publishing

Presentation by *BookLeaf Publishing*

Web: www.bookleafpub.com

E-mail: info@bookleafpub.com

ISBN: 9789357440493

First edition 2023

DEDICATION

To me. For surviving.

ACKNOWLEDGEMENT

Thank you to the people in my life who showed up, spoke up, and helped out during my worst moments. While words are healing, and I look to them to keep my faith, the people in my life are the foundation holding me together. You know who you are.

Paint Streaks

I see us in color. I always have.
These vivid reds and blues and purples.
Fire and air.
Explosive even at the best of times.

When all of my world is black and white, you
walk through the door and turn it red.

I shy away from the flames.
I take cover.
We collide and break down and feel like we won't
make it out of this.

But when it's all over, I cling to you.
Because that nothing inside of me — the gray
that paints my world — suddenly looks real and
warm and close within your arms.

I lock it all inside.
Years of learning how not to feel.
It all comes crashing down when you enter the
room.
And it hurt just as much every time I lost you.
Plunging my world into cool tones of
desperation.

I keep coming back because your colors call me
to you.
I find that I want to live life within the paint
streaks of your love.
They warm me in ways that no other ever has.
The city I call home.

Panic

I grab a bag of rice
The cans of beans — 5.
     No, 8.
All that's left on the empty shelves of this
armageddon scene.

I call my mom.
     3x.
I roll the dice and take the subway to my office.
Grab the last remaining things of the life I used
to live. Like a monitor and keyboard will help
me survive this.

Watch the empty streets below turn hollow and
haunted.

We order in, stare at each other through screens,
and go through wine like water.

I think about the distance I can no longer travel.
The plans we no longer have.
A world that looks different — smaller, harder
     With every passing day
I try not to fill myself with what-ifs and
nightmares.

But my anxiety is tenfold.
My heart is always beating fast.
If this goes on much longer I don't know that I
can last —
       Alone in these four walls
       500 square feet
And a window that faces brick.

For all the city girl in me, I still long for the
fresh air, warm arms, and the familiar scent of
rain on dirt.

That's how my bags end up packed, just like the
carts in the grocery store.

Brave

Everyone always tells me I'm brave
    Courageous
    Strong
    Bold
    Brilliant
I can change my life like some people change
clothes. Strip one identity for another. Make
copies of new keys and sell everything I own.

Just to buy it all again.

I take leaps of faith
I trust my gut
I hustle and girl boss and stand strong (still my
knees are shaking)

But this was different.

I picked a place and dug a space for my roots to
grow. To plant trees I couldn't pull up.
Watch the branches reach the sky
Feel the roots burrow deeper into the earth — a
physical reflection of what it is to be loved.

This time I wanted stability
        A home
        Belongings I didn't want to get rid
        Happiness and hope
        Peace and ease

This time I wanted to live one singular life.
I didn't want to be brave. I wanted to be home.

I've been running for lifetimes.

One life after the other until they all start blending together.

In one, I was running through the forest, clinging to a man that felt like home. Branches crushed under feet, the brush tearing at my dress, leather sandals not enough to protect my fragile skin from the elements.

We are running for freedom. For our lives. Voices and arrows spring to life behind us. Our enemies are close behind.

My hair is matted to my forehead — the result of sweat and tears. Blood coats my arms and legs. I can't remember what I've done, but it was enough to send the troops after me.

And then it happens.

A piercing arrow punctures the soft skin just below my rib cage. Searing straight through me.

It should kill me, but it doesn't. This is not the first arrow to narrowly miss my heart. There's a map of scars on my broken body left by the others that aimed and missed.

Still, it won't be the last.

He grabs me as I fall and, with all his desperation, forces me out of the woods, through the thicket, into the open.

I'll die. I know. But it doesn't seem to matter.

Because as the terror comes to an end, I am wrapped in the arms of a safe place. A familiar being. A precious scent. A person who braved shots fired just to get us to freedom.

In this life, I'm standing in a dark alley by myself. Sobbing into my hands. Scared of being rescued.

The lies I'll have to tell to hide what's been done. The story I need to weave to hide my shame.

Sixteen and alone — because the world I grew up in taught only toxic love and the powerlessness of weakness.

In this life, no one is running to protect me from fired shots. Helping me to the other side.

In this life, they hit me over and over again with sharp arrows and wicked tongues. Chip away at my voice. My worth. My spirit.

I want to tell her that her voice is worth hearing. That she should have started screaming and making a scene. She should have lit every match until Newport Beach burned so bright that even Los Angeles could feel her heat.

And I want to tell her that it's not her fault she couldn't speak — but I will. For both of us.

I'll carry her to the other side now.

How did I get here?

3,000 miles away on this windswept ocean?

The cold freezes the tears as they fall
The grey never turns and the colors that once
stained my world are beginning to fade. A
memory I can barely hold onto.

How did I get here?
Scared to walk the street past 8 PM
Desperate for a friend that doesn't talk about
hiking or camping
A cocktail with flair
A gas station with an attendant
A place where a pitched tent isn't an omen
you'd rather turn away from.

How did I get here?
This dank and desolate coastal town — full of
people who hate me
Hate outsiders.
The seals never stop and neither do the
backhanded compliments
No culture and no love despite the signs on their
lawns.

A society that destroys all unfamiliar things.
(bigots, misogynists, racists, oh my.)

The same people that would walk the streets of
my city looking for a good time and a fast high
Like we don't hate how slow they move on our
sidewalks
How long it takes them to order a fucking bagel
How uninformed and removed they are from our
ever-changing world.

Still, we smile and serve them
We welcome them with open arms — however
urgent and fast that may seem.
Stay in your hometown where you belong, we
should say.
But we won't.

How did I get here?
Stamped with the brand of failure that never
goes away
Looking at the blank canvas of my future
without a paintbrush.
Lost. Lost. Lost.

How did I get here?

How do I get out?

Heaven…

Do you know how much it aches? The memory of you?

No.

If you did you never would have left for bluer skies and greener pastures.

You would have survived the pain so I could forgo mine.

Or left blood stains and bad deeds behind to keep the past a danger sign.

You never would have loved so hard and left me with this empty reminder of how it feels. That love. A love I'll never have again.

It doesn't exist outside of your grace.

If you knew how much it ached…
        If you knew my heart would break…

Would heaven have seemed a better place?

Astoria, Oregon

You should know what the villain in the tale
looks like — your city runs on the profits from
the story.

I hope I left a mark on you as you did on me.
Bruised blue and purple and pink.
I hope you spend a lifetime trying to rub it out.

Out damn spot.
Out damn spot.
Out.

Insomnia

Tonight will not be one of those nights. I'm
getting into bed and turning off the lights. I'm
listening to the ocean waves crashing and
drawing themselves back out to sea. I'm quieting
my mind and breathing slowly.

The next thing I know, I'm thinking of that thing
I said two hours ago or how I can't speak what's
on my mind when I feel it the most. I'm shaking
my foot as I sit at the edge of the bed and staring
down at the pills in my hand — a lover I can't
seem to quit because she wraps me so tightly in
her grip. I shake one out at 1 AM and swear it
will work. This time.

I do the whole routine only to be staring at the
ceiling at 3 AM. I'm thinking about everything I
said and did and how much it might have stung.
I'm replaying all the memories. I hope I can
time-travel back and fix the words. I'm
wondering why it always comes to this with me
and where the flaw in my humanity went so off
course. I don't pray because I don't believe in

God, but I'm desperate for something to help me change this tired routine.

I shake one more pill out at 4 AM and finally fall into the dark. I can't say it's restful, but it shuts it all off. And even though I swore I wouldn't avoid the racing thoughts and underlying panic attacks, I'm thankful for the reprieve. Sometimes letting the darkness suck you in is the only joy you need.

Midnight

I gather myself, or what's left of me at that midnight, and climb into a car.

I drive for miles. Until this city that I don't know, that doesn't know me, and all of its silly idiosyncracies, fade into the distance of my review mirror. I whisper goodbye. Imagine the joy of fulling leaving it behind.

I listen to songs with words I don't understand. I trust in a map I've never looked at before. I stop at an outlook that juts out over the cliffside facing east. And I imagine the lighthouse on the opposite coast calling to me. Pulling me in. Wanting be back. Asking me home.

And I try not to miss it.

It wasn't the end of the world, but it sure felt like it.

Blood, sweat, tears
    Bones chipped with an ice pick
    My body flayed open
    My mind turned to blank spaces filled with
ghosts who haunt all my waking moments.

Everything aches
    All the time with no relief
    No pain killer on earth can get to the
brainstem.
    Heavy on the scale and in my heart.

That's how it feels when stripped of your dignity
again and again.

All these people on the sidelines
    In the stands
Watching me lose everything
Witnessing the fall of who I was
Who I am
How I stopped breathing from choking on my own
dreams
Are you laughing with glee?

It wasn't the end of the world.
But I think I died anyway.

8/22/22

I stopped taking all my medication a few weeks ago.

All I know is that nothing has been right since I started trying to fix my wrongs.

All I know is each failure has hit harder than the last — spilling my tears and blood across a canvas I can't repaint.

All I know is I've felt sick and tired.
Lost and abandoned.
No matter how much I try to be healthy and happy and normal.

All I know is I left behind a life that made sense for complete madness.

All I know is I don't know anything anymore. And I can't keep trying to figure it out.

What comes will come — and all I know is I want to be myself when it ends.

I can envision it.

I can envision what it would be like to let go of the ties that bind me to the past and fully give myself over to someone new.

I can imagine what it would be like to let someone back in. Breathe through the fear and the remnants of pain, expose the nerves, and let someone see me again. To fully trust what a person says is also what they'll do.

That authenticity isn't a leftover idea from simpler days when people cared more about loving the people who love them back than loving those who don't even know them.

I'm waiting to believe in trust again, to fully give myself over to another person without constantly wondering, worrying, and rushing.

To put my heart, battered and bruised as it might be, right into their hands and have faith they'll care for it. That the scars will fade, and I can be whole. That I can be loved despite the mistakes I've made and the flaws I have. Despite the damage done to me.

I can see it.

Right there on the horizon.

Like a photograph of some faraway town you
dream of walking through someday.

I just don't know if I can get there.

Bad therapy.

It's 4 PM and all I want to do is open a bottle and keep pouring glasses until it's gone. I know it's insane to fret about drinking early in the day, but you sliced me open from the inside out just this morning. I need a first aid kit to numb the pain, and alcohol seems to be the only tool available. It's right here on my table. No ER, no doctors, no one to strap me to a gurney, shuffling me into an ambulance.

You told me not to drink because I need to feel the softness, the broken pieces, the tears in my heart.

But feeling it makes me angry. Anger makes me reckless. And I'm afraid of who I'll be if I let myself sink into it.

Like right now. I'm mad at you for letting this all come to the surface. For poking and prodding me until the words and tears spilled over. My whole body hurt with pain, and I doubled over in my car, trying to stop the tears. A wound that can't stop gushing blood. A live wire. So scared someone would see me as I came undone in the front seat, hat pulled down over my eyes, body shaking with the force of the pain.

Why leave me exposed to the elements? Just as the winter starts rolling in, you open me up, strip me bare, and toss me outside without a coat. How the fuck am I going to survive this if all you do is remove every remaining shred of dignity I have. Reflect my self-doubt back at me. Ask questions I don't have answers to.

Just tell me I'm fucked up, and let me leave. Tell me there's no helping me. Don't make it worse. Don't make it hurt. Don't leave me at the bottom of this well, thirsty and aching. Don't you know that's when I react? Don't you know that's how I learned to sew myself back into my armor, heavier-handed than the time before? Don't you know that's how I've ruined myself?

You're supposed to be helping me, and all I feel is hopeless. All I want is alcohol. I want to feel nothing. Be nothing. Want nothing.

So let me open this bottle and drown myself in it.

Sometimes when the rain falls, I still think about you.

Iron fire escapes look out over brick buildings and
backyards
Into the windows of unsuspecting city dwellers
who never think about those of us interested in the
private lives of others
A pillow leans back against the window sill
Holding my weight
Holding my dreams
As the muted stars dance above me in the night sky
Blinded by the neon and bright lights below
Voices echo in the air from the bars below
But we hear nothing
It's just the two of us here
Filled with the wonder of all that could be
Would be
Should be
Maybe nothing will come from this, but at least I
have this moment
Being one with you and all the things that make
you buzz
I am the most alive I've ever been

Vessel

They say the body is sacred

Mine feels like a vessel that destroys me slowly.

I feed my mind and soul and leave the wasted
leftovers for this thing that carries me.

When my mind gave up on me, and my heart
shattered — I let my body go, too.

How can I possibly live in this sacred place that
reminds me of my most terrifying nightmares?
The imprint of all of my failures?

I think… maybe
I've tried to destroy it.
All this time, it was me.
Because this body.
This temple.
This vessel.

It was the first thing to let me down.

Alter ego

What I want more than anything is for all of your words to spill out onto the floor, the letters scattering like game pieces over the hardwood, so I can pick through and assemble them.

Piece and puzzle them together. Know what you hide behind the long silences as we breathe in sync in the dark.

If I could craft the words just right, maybe it would erase the scrawl of obscenities written inside my skull. Graffiti left behind by lost lovers, broken promises, unfinished business, and the shame of being the gasoline-fueled wandered I am.

I don't want these games of Scrabble to be just a memory I eventually write across my heavy bones. Or a reminder of the steps not being taken. The bed not being slept in. The clean oxygen I'm not breathing when you leave long enough for me to press another nicotine-filled moment to my lips.

I want the beauty of the words you keep inside to stain my skin like a tattoo. Written in forever.

Fused glass

I used to look at myself like I was shattered glass. This person who left shards and pieces of herself everywhere she went.

I said, "Here, take this piece, I don't need it anymore." And you carved it out with the sharp talons on your fingertips.

A destructive force who only wanted to splinter the edges of who I am. You tapped at the fragile glass and shook the ground beneath my unsteady foundation until you left your mark all over me.

So, take it.
Take all the pieces that make me whole.
I was born broken anyway.

I was too young to know the difference.

But as I got older, I realized that those small splintered pieces of my soul weren't gone. There were cracks, and I was shattered. But somewhere along the way, somehow, I'd managed to glue all those missing parts back together.

And I didn't need anyone to gift me back what I'd
given away. I didn't need those ghosts of my past
to give me permission to be whole. I was whole. I
had made myself that way.

And now I see…
 there's something about fused glass that's more
beautiful, anyway.

California

I never thought I'd cross your borders again.
My self-exile was a permanent ban.
I walled myself off and away.
You were the link to the past I wanted to forget.
To protect my heart, I needed to say goodbye.

But after everywhere else tried to destroy me,
there was only one way back to myself.

To let the sun shine on my skin the only way
California rays can.

So here I am. At your door. I won't beg, but this
time…
I'll stay.

Please let me in.

Sunset Beach

I just unpacked my boxes.
Another new home, the fourth in a year.
The backyard overlooks the bay and I look up at
the sky as I remind myself to breathe.
Purple, pink, blue, red — it's the sunset of so
many dreams.
People come to California for this.
I see the beauty. I see the novelty.
But…
I see something else.
I see a new beginning.
The birth of dreams I didn't know I had back
then.
A backyard filled with friends.
Friends I took years to let in.

I see courage.
I see hope.
Mostly, I see that letting go is the most freeing
feeling I've ever known.
Despite everything, I think I'm finding faith in
my heart again.

Hi I love you

Once a city of skyscrapers coated in glass and
gray and black.
An east village apartment that found me when I
was on the verge of falling apart.
The bar on Avenue A, where I learned to drink
hard liquor and have snowball fights in the park
with strangers.

Even in the dead of a desolate winter, there is
color everywhere.
I walk up Mercer to that spot in the Bowery, and
I see the colors in the shop windows. We wander
down Spring Street on the weekends and pass
The Little Prince. Full of flowers, bright purples,
and pinks. How is something so urban this
beautiful in my eyes?

There's something in me I can't deny blooms
when my soul's axis lands on this latitude. Even
when I left that final time, as the streets emptied
and the shelves cleared, I knew I was marked
and scarred by this place. I knew the love I felt
would hum inside me forever.

Today it all ended.

It wasn't the big sweeping, explosive departure I
hoped for
It was silent and quiet
Slipping out the back door of a party while the
music still rages behind you
I didn't say any goodbyes
Or send out any texts

It ended like it began
Uncertain, sudden, crystal clear

The Uhaul truck in the review mirror, cats
sleeping in the back, we crossed from Oregon to
California and unpacked.

I'm the where's waldo of drifters.
Blink, and you miss him.

But today, it's over.
I cut the final thread to a past that strangled me
with rope.
I said goodbye and let it go.
I washed my hands clean and lifted myself up.

I stopped turning to the North and focused on moving South.
Somewhere warmer. Somewhere calmer.
A place I used to call home.
Maybe it can be again.

I honestly don't know what will happen next.

It could be epic and brilliant, or it could fizzle fast.
But as of today, this moment, right now.
I'm not clinging to the past.